The
LADDER

A Fable About the Power of Writing

JASON HOUSER

Using your personal powers
of choice and writing
to guide you during dark times
and change your life forever.

Dedicated to those who have experienced
devastating circumstances in life,
hoping that they too could use their own
ladder (choice) and path (writing)
to receive a refreshing healing,
from this book and
their own efforts to heal.

Produced by BookCreate
Redmond, Washington USA

Printed in USA

Table of Contents

Introduction

In which I welcome you to our fable and share
with you what to expect.

*"When we least expect it, life sets us a challenge to
test our courage and willingness to change; at such a
moment, there is no point in pretending that nothing
has happened or in saying that we are not yet ready.
The challenge will not wait. Life does not look back."*
– Paulo Coelho

**Fables are stories meant to teach the reader a les-
son.** That's the definition according to a great many
different sources. I don't like the phrase 'teach you a
lesson'. It sounds harsh, brusque, and that's not what
I'm going for at all. In fact, quite the opposite. I am
gently placing the knowledge before you and humbly
asking you to accept it into your life. The truth is that I
started writing the fable featured between these pages
when I was at a low point in my life. I reached my own
metaphorical rock-bottom and had to claw myself back
out of the cavern I found myself tempted to stay in. I
know that so many of you out there will have reached

your own lowest point, maybe you're there now, and I feel that it is with great purpose that I give you this word picture to aid in making your own climb out of the abyss as easily as possible. I am providing you a ladder through which to climb out of your rock bottom. The ladder is writing. They are one and the same. Writing is a tool to get you out of rock bottom and into the light again. Festering in a dark place can only lead to us becoming more jaded, and it is in our best interest to do all we can to return to our lives, having left our troubles behind at the bottom of the cavern.

The fable I will share with you tells the story of one man's journey. It is a metaphor for my life, for the lives of all the people out there who have gone through struggles and come out on the other side. It is no easy feat by anyone's standards. No matter what knocks you down, getting back up again takes strength. But more than that, it takes an understanding of your wounds and scars, an understanding of the healing process. Because that's the thing isn't it? With mental wounds and scars, other people can't see them and therefore they feel less real. It's not as simple to heal as a broken leg in a cast, or a cut sewn together. Troubles of the mind are harder to fix, but not impossible. These wounds and scars can prevent us from moving forward. They can even make us think we don't want to progress, that we're perfectly happy to stay as we are, but that is detrimental, too. It's called denial. If something in your past that left a scar on your mind, prevents you from evolving and progressing, it is imperative that you do all you can to heal the scar. It is something especially magical about humans, our ability to evolve within our lives, to grow as people, and become wise. Not doing so leads to stagnation, and I'm sure you agree, it is impossible to be truly happy if you are stagnant.

This isn't a typical self-help book in which I tell you that journaling can change your life. No, it's a self-action book where I show you that writing (maybe that's journaling) can change your life. The simple act of picking up a pen and scrawling words on a piece of paper is therapeutic. Those letters and symbols you write onto the page have meaning. Meaning stemming from your mind, your brain, your unconscious thought. Whether you are writing a list, a novel, or in a journal, the fact that we as humans are able to transfer our thoughts to paper sets us apart as a species. Surely this is not by accident. I don't believe it is at least. We have been given this gift, 'the pen is mightier than the sword' as they say, to transfer our deepest thoughts and beliefs into marks on a page and that is no less than enchanting. Words themselves have the power to change the world, so it should go without saying that words can heal your wounds and change your life. *"Words have energy and power with the ability to help, to heal, to hinder, to hurt, to harm, to humiliate, and to humble."* -Yehuda Berg. To me, words are living, breathing entities and when we write them on a page, the energy is passed from us and into the world. It doesn't matter whether there's anyone out there willing to read what you've written, the important thing is that you've written words.

Our book will start with a fable. The following chapter contains the aforementioned fable. Read between the lines as you take the journey into, and out of, the chasm. After that, we'll get to the self-action portion of the book, with simple and natural ways to make writing work for you. I am not one to prescribe a specific arbitrary method to something as subjective as writing and journaling. What I will give you is a selection of different adaptations that you might choose to try - writing in different ways but with two main purposes. To heal and grow. Writing is our tool. How we choose to use the tool is our own prerogative. But the outcome is always the same. Healing and growth. Writing heals wounds, burns bridges to past pains, and pushes us forth into our futures. How you choose to use this book is up to you. I hope that you take the lessons to be learned and apply them to your own life, adapting them for your needs. What I share with you is my truth and my truth alone, a journey I went on with the purpose of healing. Through this journey, I found my calling… being a catalyst of growth to others. I am here as your humble guide, giving you the tools to overcome whatever obstacles you have faced, and equipping you for the future. It is an honor to accompany you as such.

Our Fable

Where I share with you the power of writing as a tool to overcome the most challenging of situations.

"You have power over your mind
– not outside events.
Realize this, and you will find strength."
– Marcus Aurelius

This word picture, as I like to call it, forms the key part of the book. Not only is this an example to learn from, but it is an example of how the process of writing can heal. As I encourage you to start your writing journey, this is a part of my own writing journey. The following fable is what came to me in one of my great moments of desperation, while I was grasping at straws to find my purpose. Seated in front of a plain piece of paper, pen in hand, this is what flowed from within me. It was a natural experience, as natural as breathing. But that does not mean it was easy. As I wrote I came across problems. Writer's block, busy schedules, deep emotions, and real-life, painted a grey cloud over the process at times. Like the metaphor in the fable below, I overcame these battles. There is no excuse for not writing if you want to do it, not one that's valid, anyway.

This fable is the start of something. It means a lot to me. It is a picture of human choice, and process, and healing, and opportunity. Think of the ladder, think of the pen, think of your own lives. Here we go.

The Ladder, the Path and the Water

Like a painfully wounded bird I hobble, the cold anguish from many previous hurts slows my limbs. The haunting memories of my soul's pain pushes me on through a desolate desert in search of a place of escape or rest. My blurred vision picks up barely any sign of life in this lonely place. Gritty sand and old mud muffle the hollow thump as my foot strikes ever so gently. This new residence that I find myself helplessly lost in is so horrible and so vastly threatening that it consumes the shriveled hope I hold so dear. As I stagger through the swirling dust beginning to obsess about my pain and suffering, I come upon a new sight. A short distance away I behold what looks like the end of everything. Like a fringe at the end of the desert abutted to another realm, my weakened determination urges me forth at a snail's pace to investigate what I might be seeing. In a near slumber, I work my way to the brink of a sharply cliffed canyon. The fear-filled air makes the hair on my neck stand firm. The darkness that surrounds this cliff is almost unbearable. Butterflies churn in my stomach. It is the crest of a vast canyon containing unfathomable darkness. The depth of the pit alone masks all perceptions of its final hidden power. I consider it a place of possible escape from this undesirable desert journey, but I can't see how deep it will go or how dark it will get. Its width is so far-reaching that the other side of the canyon seems like a fantasy. It appears beautiful and spectacular but so far out of reach. Inching closer, I carefully lean in toward the darkness to ponder whether there is relief in this oddly familiar pit. I am fully exhausted. I sway back and forth almost losing my balance. Emotional weariness is the only description I have for what I am experiencing. Just plain weary. Then something catches my eye to my left.

I turn my tired eyes toward the object. What! I see what looks like a pile of branches. The thick tree branches are tightly woven together by twine and combine to make a sturdy ladder. "Why in God's good name would there be a handmade ladder in the middle of the desert near a bottomless pit of darkness?" I think to myself. It lies there as though it was hastily placed near the edge by someone prior to me who tried to realize its use to no avail. "Surely nobody would just jump into the all-consuming pit no matter how enticing the escape may be," my weak voice denotes. As for myself, I oddly comprehend the possibility of doing just this. My back and neck tighten intensely at the thought. The pit appears like a valid option to escape this pain. "Just jump in," I tell myself as shivers go down my body. Then I look at the wooden ladder, taking my turn to realize its usefulness. I think to myself, "I can use this ladder to gradually go down into this canyon of darkness while still giving myself a way to escape at any moment if I get overwhelmed by anxiety." (The ladder represents my CHOICE despite my hurt and pain). Remembering past personal ventures into other canyons of my life, I realize something quite quickly. The ladder, when lowered down, would disappear into the darkness and I would fall with it into despair. I could not see anything to trust the ladder's stability, and so the ladder would be useless for this half-hearted venture into the abyss. As this realization hits and I ponder the act of just going in because it is the easiest way to escape my pain, I notice a slowly flowing fresh water river far in the distance across the canyon.

There is a special feeling about this river. I am drawn to it from my innermost being. Hope rises up from it with beauty, but it is so far away from this horrible place that I now stand. I would have to cross the dark pit to get to it. Even further in the distance to my left, I see the river, as tiny as it looks, creeping its way along the canyon to a point where the canyon narrows. Hope opens my eyes briefly enabling me to see a dirt path meandering along the dark side of the canyon. (This path represents my writing). The emergence of this hope-filled path changes the usefulness of my newly discovered ladder (choice). The ladder can help me in a different way even though it is the same ladder. If I just take a short journey on the path down the edge of this pit I can use the ladder to make it to the other side and skip the darkness altogether. So, I muster up all my strength and do it. I pick up the ladder to commence my journey down the path.

As I walk the pit gets smaller, not as wide, not all-engulfing. The closer I get to the narrowest part of the canyon (by writing) the more confident I become about making the right decision to use my ladder wisely. Beyond the canyon depths on the other side, I am beginning to see signs of life. There are small trees, wonderful shrubs blowing in the breeze, and wildlife. The bubbling river is now closer than ever, but the dark cavern below still blocks much of the beauty of the other side. The bleak pit is still oddly enticing. I finally get to the spot where the canyon is at its most narrow. I position the ladder flat on the ground as to push it along the desert floor. I slightly lift it up and lay it down across the dark space. IT BARELY FITS. It is just the right ladder. I am relieved. There is a way across. There is some hope in this dark hour. I slowly inch my way on the ladder testing the strength of it. Will it hold me? Will I fail to make it across? I slowly make my way across my bridge while the darkness below becomes heavier and heavier. I pause with fear. "Maybe I can't make it." I think to myself. I look down to see what this pit really is and find that I cannot see a thing. Though narrower, it is still so deep and dark that no sense can be made of it. Then I feel my first shot of warmth. The glimmer of sunlight touches down on my neck from the other side. It feels good. I turn to keep moving and can see the inner edges of the cliff on the other side because the sun is moving in the sky. I can only see a small amount of it, but it is more revealing than any other moment thus far. I realize that the pit is no place that I want to stay. I move on.

Once I make it to the other side on my choice ladder, the sun shines brightly with great intensity on my face and all around me. Wow! What a different place this is. I notice that the darkness is gone because of the sun. From this side, I can see all that the canyon contains. Oh boy, is it ugly - but it was too dark to see it for what it was on the other side. Taking the path (writing) and using my special ladder (choice) to bridge the gap, I can see more clearly. Desiring to take advantage of all the sun's glory, I investigate the pit. I saw a spiral going for what seemed like miles with words on it. The words were repeated over and over while they got bigger and bigger toward the bottom. The words were anger, bitterness, unforgiveness, fear, anxiety, obsession, insecurity, self-hatred, depression, and loneliness. All the same words and emotions raging out of control and getting worse as my eyes worked down the spiral to the bottom of the pit. When my eyes met the floor of this huge crack in the earth, I noticed it was completely covered with ladders. Some of them were mine from past attempts at lowering myself in slowly. Some of them were the ladders others used to do the same. So many times, I have chosen to use my ladder to go down to that lonely place. I also discovered that the ladder did not make it easier to get out of the pit. I still had to use my ladder to get onto the spiral but I had to walk up the spiral through all of the words to get out. It looked like a long and painful process. Using the ladder to bridge the gap seemed so much wiser.

Suddenly I felt intense freedom from all that darkness but noticed something very alarming at the same moment. The words on the spiral were now inscribed on my heart and I had never noticed. The hurt and the pain were on my heart. The words could barely be seen through the hard calluses that covered them. Fear filled my soul. I had chosen not to go into the pit, but my choice didn't make the feelings of my heart disappear. In a sense I was relieved. I saw how bad the pit was and all the unneeded devastation it caused. I also saw that my journey down the path and the use of my ladder allowed me to be what I am in the present time. I had not indulged in obsessive darkness and had not tried to escape the emotions. The path and the ladder helped me to the other side of a dark hour. "What did all of this mean?" I asked myself. I was confused that the words on the spiral were on my heart even though I had bypassed the dark pit. As the sun shone ever so brilliantly it hit me. THE WATER! That water is what the path and the ladder were for. The writing and the choice were not the whole story. The pit of darkness was not the whole story. It was the water that I was after. The healing and the cleansing. So, I turned my teary eyes behind me to gaze at the beautiful flowing river. It was majestic and inviting as the rays of sun warmed its surface. Once again, I used my ladder to climb down the riverbank that was filled with thriving vegetation. It was beautiful and lively. The shrubs and flowers were so numerous that it was impossible to get to the river without going through the vegetation. It ran across my body and heart as I walked down my ladder. The branches and leaves scratched against me, yet it was not painful. I was surprised at the gentle softness that I felt. As they scraped against the painful words on my heart, the calluses were opened and prepared for the river's cleansing.

My feet hit the warm, grey sand beach. Suddenly a powerful mist spontaneously broke forth from the flowing river. It filled the air with a grotesque stench. It was horrible. I wondered why such a smell would come from such beauty. Step by step, I slowly made my way into the river. My feet, then ankles, then knees. The mist became much more intense, and I could no longer see anything around me. It was just a refreshing mist that smelled horrible. As I sat down in the shallow river I was engulfed by refreshment. I had forgotten about the dark pit. It was nowhere within me. I saw bits and pieces of callous floating away. I quickly looked at my heart. It was glorious. I could see so clearly each emotion that was on the spiral now printed on my heart in soft and supple scar tissue. My heart was no longer hard. I still contained within my heart all that I had been through, but the water had healed the wounds leaving only a clear stamp of a healing experience. The words were now healing words.

I wept and wept as more and more hardness left me. At this point, the mist began to dissipate. I looked up at the river and gazed upon the unbelievable. I could see what seemed like light-years away and the river was flowing out of my previous heart. The words pain, humiliation, insecurity, embarrassment, fat, lazy, and a plethora of other painful experiences were floating in the mist and this was the stench I was smelling. As the last one passed by, the mist subsided, and the stench was gone. The world opened up to me again. The sun still shone the same, yet the surroundings were transfigured into life. It was all so much clearer than before when my heart was hard. It was quiet and only the river moved and made a sound.

I arose from the river and climbed my ladder back up to the top of the riverbank. Oh, what a sight it was.

The canyon had closed in so that my ladder could cross at any point along the path. As long as I was writing (the path) and remembered that I had a choice(the ladder) to not go down into the pit, I could cross over to get fresh water. So refreshed and humbled, I turned my head slowly to the right. It was another grotesque sight. It was another dark canyon. I was almost destroyed by fear and anxiety yet again, but my heart had changed. Then I saw it, a ladder resting on a stump at the widest part of the newly discovered canyon. What a soothing sight it was! Even though the new pit would come with its own hurt and pain I still had my ladder. Leading from the stump, a dirt pathway led to the narrowest part of the new canyon. It looked like many had walked it before me. I remembered it was not so much about the pathway or the ladder but the water. I peered into the distance again to find the refreshing water. I saw the river and, in its mist, carried the words of the pain and hurt that was just previously on my heart slowly floating toward the narrow spot. I took my notebook and my choices, raised my head to the heavens, and thanked God for what he had just taught me by showing me the new canyon.

I didn't have to be afraid anymore. I was just who I am. That healing is always available to me and that love was there for me. I was lovable. But I needed my ladder, His special gift of choice to me, to get to the healing. That I might use it to go to the pit but that I didn't have to. And most of all, it was not the ladder or the path, or the water that was the greatest gift of all. **The greatest gift of all was the opportunity to use them.**

I hope that you see yourself in this fable. I don't mean that I hope you've faced terrible pains and mental anguish. But I mean that I hope you see yourself as strong enough to overcome whatever pains you have previously faced. That you know you can heal. The phrase 'time heals all wounds' is not always the case unless you take action with tools that can help you. Time, without any action, only leads to stagnation. Picking up your pen and starting to write as a tool to heal enables you to evolve. If you are able to, take some time to reflect on your feelings regarding the story I have told. Maybe pick up a pen and paper and write about it. Even something as simple as writing about the emotions you felt while reading, or what you interpret the fable to mean can get the creative writing juices flowing. With that being said, shall we take a foray into my advice about how to make writing work for you?

The Real-Life Applications of a Fable

In which I share how to make writing work for you.

"There is a saying in Tibetan,
'Tragedy should be utilized as a source of strength.'
No matter what sort of difficulties,
how painful experience is, if we lose our hope,
that's our real disaster."
– Dalai Lama XIV

The word 'writing' is one we use every single day. It's a simple word that doesn't hold a lot of emotion. It's ironic to me that a word as mundane as 'writing' can have such an impact on a person's life. That the simple act of writing can be the one thing to change a person's life when the odds seem to be ever against them. Again, I'm talking from experience here. At the time in my life when I wrote this fable; I was suffering badly. I'd been betrayed by somebody close to me, in addition to other things that kept me wanting to go down into the pit, and I didn't see a way forward from the slump

I was in. For a while, I thought that the life I was living currently was all I was ever going to be able to experience. But then something clicked within and I realized that through the betrayal and strife I'd faced, I was being given a chance at another life. This truly amazing realization came to me as I was pouring my heart out into my journal. So cliche, I know, but it's true. I was sitting there and feeling sorry for myself, which you are allowed to do, by the way. You can feel sorry for yourself, but you can't stay in that place forever. Eventually, you must choose to move on and live the life you deserve and desire. So, journaling and writing were of supreme importance at that time to understand and grow from what could have been a life-threatening experience. When I say 'life threatening' I don't mean to sound hyperbolic. I know it sounds a little extreme. But I could quite easily have let this betrayal ruin my life, blaming somebody else for the way my life had wound up. By no means would I have been the first to do this.

I poured everything I felt into my journal. The good, the bad, and the ugly. Some things that are just for my own eyes, and other things I would quite happily share. Eventually, throughout this process, I noticed the sting of emotions lessen. Eventually, everything didn't seem so raw. That was when I realized the power of writing. Writing had been a therapeutic process for me, without me even realizing it could be. Just the process of acknowledging everything I was feeling, entirely without judgment of myself because I never planned to show anybody else what I'd written, allowed me to begin to pick up the pieces of my shattered heart and heal. Very hard it was, but it was also one of the most exciting and powerful growth times of my life. I learned that you can't control people, everyone gets to do what they want to do, and you get to do what you want too. We are in charge of ourselves and how we react. That's all we can do. It is intrinsic, it comes from within. The moment our happiness and sanity depend wholly on outside factors is the moment we need to take a step back and reflect on why that is. Writing is a self-discovery tool as much as it is a tool for healing, something I will explore with you throughout the remainder of this book.

Back to Basics and the Benefits

Let's start with the general housekeeping in terms of writing. The things you need to know before we begin. First things first, there is no right way to write. There is no wrong way to write. Just as there are no right or wrong reasons to write. Whether you are writing for your eyes only, or you plan to write the next bestseller, none of that matters. What does matter is that you are doing it, you are writing, you are practicing it. You see, I believe that writing has the power to tap into our subconscious and expand our lives. It opens a door to the other side if you will. A door that allows us to work through feelings, emotions, and past experiences without even realizing that that is what we're doing. We might be aware that writing is therapeutic, but the process is something that happens within us in an almost effortless fashion. We start the process of writing, and our brain and mind do the rest. I believe some of the great philosophers of the world felt much the same about writing too.

"All I need is a sheet of paper
and something to write with,
and then I can turn the world upside down."
– Friedrich Nietzsche.

Think about this quote for a second. Philosophy and writing go hand in hand. I'm not saying that you need to become a philosopher to write. In fact, I'm saying the opposite. To become a philosopher, you have to be able to write. Philosophy and writing are one and the same. In fact, we all have a philosophy about life and what philosophy you take on will have a major impact on the outcomes in your life. Our own words reflect our inner world, our opinions, morals, values, philosophy; that part of us that is deep within. That part of us that we act from. The act of allowing your own personal philosophy to evolve through the process of writing is what writing is all about. The process of writing is about your personal connection with the world around you and your deep authentic self. Whether you are writing a diary or a novel, writing is a way to process all aspects of your life while helping yourself evolve to the next level.

You don't need to sit and write for hours and hours for it to be an enlightening experience. Even writing for a few minutes a day, and forging a habit, can have such powerful results that it can set you on a path of great adventure. For myself, and many other writers, the process of sitting down in a quiet space and writing is almost a meditative practice. Whether you prefer to sit down and write for extended periods, or you pick up a pen and spend a short while writing, it doesn't matter. What does matter is finding what works for you and building a habit of it. It's always the habit that counts. The benefits of writing are hard to ignore. We've talked already about how I used writing as a tool for healing past traumas. As with most things regarding the mind, there is no one empirical reason as to why writing helps us. It has been suggested that the experience of writing helps you to clarify thoughts and feelings, somewhat like a therapist, or a best friend would, except writing can be there for you 24/7. A journal allows you to express yourself without fear of judgment. You can pour out even your most toxic feelings and emotions, pushing them out into the world in a safe way. You don't need to be writing explicitly about your hard experiences for this to happen either. All our past experiences make us who we are today and when we write, our thoughts and feelings are an expression of this. Incorporating journaling into your healing process can bring about powerful change in an easy way.

First of all, it's a cheap and effective method. You don't need to spend a fortune on fancy gadgets when you can pick up a pen and a notepad for next to nothing. Just as talking to a friend or therapist allows you to express yourself, writing in a journal allows your feelings to flow from within you, releasing any trapped energy that causes harm within you. This reminds me of the most beautiful quote by Shakti Gawain, *"The more light you allow within you, the brighter the world you live in."* This quote just about epitomizes what it means to me to write. You create a space within you for lightness by letting go of the negative energy within you. Journaling is a great tool for releasing these negative energies. What's even better is that it's not always a conscious process. Of course, you consciously decide to write, but those feelings work their way out from within you and onto the page by themselves. The pen is the conduit.

Other than healing, writing also has other benefits that are worth being aware of. It's like getting a great bargain on your shopping… you write to heal and get loads of other benefits too. What's not to love?

1. Improving your self-confidence. This is key to healing too. By learning to love yourself and value yourself, you are far more likely to be able to move on from past struggles. By exploring your thoughts and feelings through writing, you get to know yourself better, feeling secure in your thoughts and actions. Having the confidence to say, "Yes, this happened, and because of that I am who I am today. What

happened in the past does not define me," is the most amazing feeling, believe me.

2. Improving your self-awareness. It might surprise you to realize how much of our strife is caused by poor self-awareness. Through writing, you can gain a greater level of understanding about yourself and who you are as a person. This phenomenon allows you to be more aware of your beliefs, thoughts, and reasons behind your actions. It also helps you live consciously in the moment more often

3. Better coping with current aspects in your life. Writing is not just about healing from past wounds, it's also about working through the here and now. There is a reason that journaling is used by so many mental health profession- als as part of the therapy process - because it works! Remembering that your journal is a judgment free zone, you can often express things you would struggle to say aloud, even to a therapist. Taking the time out of your busy schedule to check in with how you're feeling, how your day is going, and anything else you feel the need to get down on paper gives you moments of clarity. In terms of mental health, which I won't go on and on about, I think that could be a whole other book, journaling can help you to track your emotions and mental well-being, identifying triggers, and keeping track of symptoms, changes, and recovery. We'll cover this in a little more detail later on in this chapter.

4. Other benefits include improved cognitive functioning, problem-solving skills, and re- duced stress. Writing requires your brain to be alert, but in a controlled and calm way, which keeps those neurons healthy and firing as they should be. As writing is mostly a mental task, it

keeps our brains ticking nicely. When it comes to problem-solving skills, keeping a journal of sorts allows us to tease out different problems, coming to the best solution. It can help us to think with our hearts or our heads, depending on the situation. This exploration of various outcomes is worth its weight in gold when you have big decisions to make. This in turn helps to reduce stress about the future. Writing and getting our emotions out on paper can lead to a feeling of calm which can be of great use to a lot of us!

So, to come to a simple conclusion, journaling and writing is awesome and you should totally do it! But then there's the question of 'how' you should start your writing practice. Don't worry, I won't leave you hanging there, as this is the part of journaling and writing I feel puts the most people off. They don't know how to start and therefore they never do, missing out on all that valuable life changing potential.

Starting Your Writing Practice

Starting your writing practice is possibly the start of a great healing journey. We all have past experiences we could get some healing from, even if we don't know specifically what these experiences are. As we have already talked about, human beings are a combination of their past experiences. Some of these will be positive, some negative, some neutral. They are all learning experiences. I'm not saying that you have to immediately see the silver lining in every cloud, that's the amazing thing about writing. You don't have to put on a false positive front or a mask. Instead, let writing happen through you in the present moment. Whether you're angry, tired, happy, sad, or anything else, just the process of getting those words out of your brain and into the world can help you to work through whatever it is you need to.

Picture this, if you will. You're sitting in front of a blank sheet of paper, pen in hand, and you're thinking, "What the heck am I supposed to write?" This feeling is what discourages many people from writing before they have even given it a fair try. If this is you, don't feel defeated. So many others fall at the first hurdle and then give up. They miss out on the true power that journaling and writing can add to their lives. Overcomplicating matters will just lead to a stressful experience and writing is supposed to be the exact opposite to that. It's supposed to be enlightening, calming, and productive. Consider this quote from Ernest Hemingway, *"My aim is to put down on paper what I see and what I feel in the best and simplest way."* If Hemingway, one of the writers that quite literally changed the world with his craft, wants you to keep things simple, then you should! All jokes aside, writing is something simple and it should be kept that way.

I would like you to start off with something simple. Why would you like to start writing? This simple question is all I want you to think about for a moment. You could even pick up your journal and write about it if you were so inclined. You see, the reason I ask this is simple. Your intentions can lead to different outcomes. For example, if you're writing just for your own eyes and the only aim for your journal is as a tool to heal, then what you write would be different than if you were writing with the aim of being a best-selling author. There's nothing wrong with wanting to be a best-selling author, it's an admirable dream, but be aware of this before you start writing. Other than that, throw every rule you've ever heard about journaling and writing out the window and find what works for you. When you see people who appear to have it easy when it comes to writing, you often compare yourself to them. It's basic human nature to compare ourselves to others, but something as special as writing is just for you. As with anything else in life, writing and journaling can take some practice. If the words don't seem to come naturally to you, and they definitely might not to begin with, you can consider a quote, a book, a song, an experience, and write about that. Even if you only write a few sentences, it's a few more sentences than you would have if you had given up. You're a few sentences closer to healing.

If you're still having a moment of panic about the blank page in front of you, consider this... Some of the most successful people in the world journal. Possibly one of the best ways to start, is little and often. A sentence a day will do it. Committing to this for a few weeks is enough to form a habit. Once you've become comfortable with the act of writing regularly, then you can progress to different things if you want to. Remember, that even one sentence today will build up into a manuscript if that's what you desire. One sentence a day is also enough for you to see a pattern of thoughts or behaviors. Even if you record your workouts, or your reading habits, listing accomplishments or what you're grateful for, these small acts build up into something spectacular. They form a healing, self-care habit. Nobel Prize winner Danny Kahneman suggests keeping a record of every decision you make each day, which can lead to some fantastic information for reflection and self-development. This could be quite a commitment and staggering undertaking, but you never know, it might be something that you build up to over time. What I'm getting at is that writing looks entirely different for different people and that's what makes it so fantastic! You journal in a way that helps you, I journal in a way that helps me.

Free writing is a personal favorite of mine. There are a few different journaling techniques out there if you feel that you need something a little more prescriptive to help you on your way; however, free writing is the one I am most drawn to and find myself doing more often. This is the classic type of journaling that most people do without even realizing it. Basically, it means that you write whatever comes to your mind. Ideally, your pen should never leave the page, you just keep writing whatever your mind is telling you. It's like a constant stream of consciousness. Some people like to set a timer and make sure they write for a certain length of time, but that's not something that suits me. Again, you do you!

Write a narrative piece of fiction. Write a novel! Remembering to add to it regularly, just start writing. Don't think too much about the plot, setting, or characters, just put the pen to the page and start writing, even if that means you start in the middle of the story, it doesn't matter. You can always circle back around at a later date and fill in the blanks.

If you're not a fiction writer, maybe try writing a blog about something you love. Or something you don't love! Nobody ever has to see your blog, just as nobody ever has to see your novel. You don't even have to open the computer, simply write a blog in your journal, by hand, and keep it for yourself. All that matters is that you're writing something.

Another option would be to write gratitude lists. This is a nice way to both start and finish your day. Basically, you list the things you are grateful for in your life. These can be huge like being grateful for a loving family or they can be very small like being grateful for a hot shower. It can really help you to push out of a negative headspace, which in turn can help with healing.

Or try writing morning pages. This practice is something that has been around for a while but has only just started receiving any attention. The morning pages method of writing is super simple, which you know I'm a huge fan of. All you do is write when you first wake up, before you touch your phone or have breakfast or anything else. You get up and write. The method behind the madness is that you write whatever comes to mind, kind of like free writing, but because you're writing first thing in the morning there's a pureness to your thoughts. You haven't had time to put your own spin to them. They're raw, full of energy, and you write about things that are truly important to you if you're thinking about them the second you wake up in the morning.

Summarizing your day is also a popular journaling method. This is what a lot of people think of when they think of journaling. They think of a teenage girl in their bedroom with glitter pens and a locked notepad writing about the trials of their day. And, essentially, that's what you're doing (minus the gel pens and locked diary unless that's what you're into). All you need to do for this method is to describe your day. You can write it out in chronological order or focus on parts of the day that held some level of significance to you. You simply summarize the day in the way that makes the most sense to you.

Journal 'prompts' are also growing in popularity, and for good reason. You can go out and buy journals that give you a prompt each day to write about. This is great for people who are just starting their journaling journey. What is fantastic, is that you can find journals (or just lists of prompts online) for lots of different purposes - from mental health to self-discovery, you can find the journal, or prompts, to suit you. It is important to note that no matter what type of prompts you use, you are still benefiting from working through past traumas and scars, even if the prompts are not specifically around healing. It's the process of writing that heals us, not the words we write. Journal prompts might include things like, "Write a letter to your past self." Or, "What's your favorite food?" They can be literally anything and everything. Prompts are a great way to mix things up or get you started if you're not quite sure how to begin.

In reality, you'll likely use a few different methods when you're writing. Some days you might feel like listing things, another day you might feel like writing a blog post. As I have said many times now, none of that matters. All that matters is that you pick up a pen and begin to write. Therefore, you release whatever negative experiences and emotions that are causing harm within you, moving forward into the rest of your life. After all, isn't that all anybody ever wants? To live a life free of old baggage. The most important thing is that you give it a go. Do what feels right to you and hold yourself accountable to keep doing it . The problem for most people is that they give up before they see any real-life benefits. Just as you don't suddenly feel better after a single therapy session, you won't suddenly have all the benefits of journaling after 10 minutes of writing. Be sensible with it and don't expect miracles straight away. Miracles come with time and, I'm sorry to tell you, hard work too. Again, its all about building a habit of writing and journal because habits make things much more effortless.

Writing to Deal with Trauma

Throughout the previous parts of this chapter, we've talked on a generic level about using writing as a way to heal the wounds and scars in the mind. But now let's talk about if there are one or two specific traumatic incidents that are causing you harm. These are incidents that you'll be aware of. You might think of them often and they might hold a lot of emotions for you. You might even find that these experiences are holding you back from doing the things you want to do with your life. Everything we have talked about so far has been focused towards working through old scars, wounds and thought patterns that impact our lives in a general way, more a culmination of different scars and wounds, rather than something more specific and detailed. A little disclaimer here before we continue, because at the end of the day your health and well-being are the most important thing in your universe (or it should be). If you are suffering with poor mental health, no matter whether this is as the result of a specific trauma or if it's something more generic, you should always seek professional help and support. Writing therapy is a powerful tool for healing, but it cannot replace proper medical intervention. It can be used alongside other treatments, but it should never replace the care of a medical professional. So please, if you are unwell with your mental health and well-being, seek help.

Dealing with a specific traumatic incident can be difficult. It can consume all your thoughts and remove the magic from your life. So, once you have taken care of any medical needs you might face as a result of the incident (both mental and physical) writing can be used as a tool to promote healing. One of the reasons I found writing to be such a great tool for me was because deep down I was embarrassed about the betrayal I'd faced in my life. This also tapped into some deep shame from my past. I found it so difficult to talk and be honest with friends and family; therefore, writing my feelings down seemed like the perfect alternative. If you fall into this category of having specific episodes of trauma that you need to work through to live your best life, then take heed of what comes next. Remember to be discerning and choose what works for you. If you try something out and find it does nothing for you, keep searching.

If you wish to overcome specific traumatic incidents and heal from the wounds caused, you might choose to write about the event. That may seem counterintuitive, but it isn't. There's science behind the reason why writing about the event helps to overcome it, which I won't bore you with, but recalling the trauma in a safe and secure environment and taking your time to see the event for what it really was, and processing the emotions and feelings, is possibly one of the best things you can do for healing. In this instance, the control is in your hands. You can stop. You can start again. You can scribble, cry, or anything else. Nobody ever needs to know or see what you've written -- that's the beauty of writing. Should you wish, you can even burn or throw away the writing afterward. Or you can save your writing to review at a later time. I love doing this, it allows me to see how far I've come. Little changes take place every single day and you might not notice that you are changing. By keeping your writing safe and reviewing it in the future, you will be able to see the growth in your healing process and hard work. It can be nice to see and recognize your growth over time. It is something we so often overlook thanks to our busy lives.

There are no rules to writing, I'm sure you're aware of that, but I wanted to just state it again before I go on to explain how writing can help you overcome trauma. Obviously, everything we've said still stands and if you don't want to write about your traumatic experience then don't. It's that simple really. But if you do feel ready to explore the trauma and work through specific events, then here are some things you might want to consider.

It's important to take your time. Do not push yourself to do too much too soon. If it feels right to you, then do it. If it doesn't, then don't. But one quick note here: writing about trauma and overcoming events that have impacted you is never an easy thing to do. You are supposed to feel some emotions and confront them, but when it becomes too much, stop and take a break. You are in control.

Try to feel the emotions writing dredges up. Don't force them back below the surface, but also don't allow them to consume you. Whatever happened cannot hurt you now. You are the boss of your own life and can experience emotions, acknowledging and feeling them, before moving on.

Let go of any expectations you have. Go in with a curious yet neutral attitude. Whatever happens, will happen. You might expect to find writing about the trauma easy, but it might be harder than you thought. Maybe you're writing and remember something you hadn't before, or you find yourself needing to write about something else. Follow your intuition and put pen to paper. That's the main thing. Begin your story where you feel you should.

End your story where you feel you should. Revisit it, or don't. The entire process is completely up to you. Listen to your own heart and mind and do what feels good and healthy.

Writing to heal from the wounds of trauma is something entirely personal and I can't tell you how to structure your writing, how often to write, or what to do with what you've written but I can say this . . . Once you've revisited the traumatic event and written whatever you need to write, it is time to look to the future too. We can the visit the past to start to heal and then finish the job by looking to the future. Remember that the trauma is over and it won't happen again. You are in control now. You could even take a moment or two to journal from some of the following prompts if that feels right to you ...

1. What are your blessings?
2. What do you appreciate?
3. What brings you joy?
4. What have you accomplished - big or small?
5. What gifts do you have in your life?

Taking a few moments to focus on the positive can help bring us back around to a better mindset, especially if we have been focusing on something heavy like healing past trauma. Your past does not determine your future, which is why looking at your present and your future can help gain some perspective. Your life is a magical thing. How lucky are you to be alive and to be you? That's what I'd like you to think about going forward. You can heal. You can overcome. You are in control.

Writing to Support Mental Well-being

With mental health diagnosis on the rise, it is important that we cover this a little bit in a book about healing. I am by no means an expert on mental health other than being somebody who has lived with plenty of mental and emotional struggles. My experience is more firsthand, and I can share with you what I found, what worked for me, and what I hope for the future. What I say is my own experience and might be very different from yours. That doesn't mean that either of our experiences is abnormal. The fact that injury to our minds and hearts impacts all of us in different ways is part of what makes it such a tricky business. Mental well-being and journaling go hand in hand in my life, yet it can often take a combination of tools to improve our mental well-being. Part of this process can come from writing. There are three main reasons why you could choose to use writing or journaling as part of your mental well-being program. First, writing can help you to gain clarity - prioritizing problems, fears, and concerns and therefore knowing what you need to heal from. You'll be surprised, as I was, how easy it becomes, through writing, to identify areas that require healing. For example, if there's something you avoid writing about, or something that you write about an awful lot, both of these factors help you to identify what is troubling you, even if you hadn't been consciously aware of any patterns in your writing.

Writing and journaling can help you to track symptoms of poor mental habits on a daily basis. This helps you to identify triggers, which you can subsequently focus on in the healing process. Even something as simple as writing a few sentences at the end of each day can show you patterns in your behavior and can lead you to hone in on what needs to be healed within you. Not only that, but the act of journaling can give you an opportunity to practice some positive self-talk. We are often so negative about ourselves in a way we would never ever be with friends and family. On a side note, when you catch yourself being negative about yourself think, "Would I say this to my loved one?" If the answer is no, then you shouldn't be saying it to yourself. Whether you use your journal to track symptoms, or for self-improvement, all of these support the healing process. Healing is about taking accountability for your own feelings and your own happiness and writing is just one way we can do that. When we struggle with our mental well-being, for whatever reason, I believe that we can lose our sense of identity. Often, we think ourselves and the mental illness are synonymous and that shouldn't be the case at all. The process of journaling or writing allows us to see ourselves as human and fallible, and accept that this is okay. We don't have to be perfect all of the time.

You might wish to try some journaling prompts for mental well-being and recovery. Below are some common journal prompts you'll come across for those wishing to concentrate entirely on their mental illnesses, whatever they might be…

Write down five things that make you feel incredibly happy. Why do they make you feel that way?

What do you fear the most? Why? Is it a rational fear?

Describe your perfect day.

Write a letter to the past/future you.

Write down a list of regrets you have. Either throw them away or decide to move on.

What do you want your future to look like? How are you going to achieve that?

There are hundreds and hundreds more online if you'd like more prompts. Simply Google 'Journal Prompts for _____.' and you'll find what you're looking for. Alternatively, you can purchase guided journals for mental well-being too, if you fancy trying that.

Again, journaling for mental health doesn't have to be any different than journaling for anything else in the world. The simple act of writing is part of the healing process. Without meaning to, you may find that you start to work through issues you never knew you had.

Our fable taught us that writing is the tool for healing, so pick up that pen and do what feels right for you. Whatever that might be.

Writing to Cope with Physical Ailments

Writing doesn't just have the power to help us heal our mental wounds and scars, but can also be used as a tool to support our physical well-being. I'm not making crazy assertions that writing can cure cancer or anything like that before you mistake my meaning. But writing is a magical thing, and believe it or not, it has been proven to help aid the healing of physical ailments, too. Whether you suffer from a chronic, ongoing condition, or something more temporary in nature, journaling and writing is something you can take upon yourself to support the healing process and understand what is happening to your physical self. In a very literal way, the process of writing can reduce stress and therefore boost your immunity, which just shows how powerful we humans are and how magical the world around us is. If something as simple as relaxing and writing can make us less susceptible and better able to fight disease, then imagine what else our mind-body connection is capable of doing. If you have a chronic illness, or an illness that makes your daily life more complicated, this can take a toll on your mental well-being. It adds an extra challenge to daily life. Writing not only helps us to cope with stress and manage situations, but it also makes us more resilient people. This comes from the reflective, calm period we have when our pen flows on the paper, looping and circling. It connects us with the spirituality inside of us, whatever that means for you. The insight that you develop as a result of journaling and writing, both of yourself and your place in the wider world, helps in many areas of life. You might choose to practice free writing or different journaling methods, as they too can help you connect with yourself; however, for those who feel they get some additional benefit from prompts, these are some you might choose to explore if you're journaling to help yourself heal from something physical.

1. Where am I feeling pain or exhaustion in my body?
2. What can I control? What is out of my control?
3. Write a letter to your body.
4. What have you endured and conquered in your life so far?
5. In what ways do your physical and mental health connect?
6. Picture yourself surrounded by joy. What would this look like?

Even when writing to aid the healing process of physical ailments, it can often be pertinent to try to look at things from a positive angle. Of course, you might not feel positive about your situation, but you can find positive things in your life to be thankful for and you can include these in your writings wherever possible. Try not to get stuck in the negatives. It is easy to do, especially if you are in pain. Dwell on the pain for a short while if you must and then look to the future.

Journaling is not a magic pill that will heal everything in your life and without any effort on your part. You still have to put the work in. Put pen to paper. Consider everything that we've spoken of so far about finding a method of journaling or writing that works for you. Stick with it. The results might not happen overnight, nothing good ever does, but it will come with time and with practice. Forming a habit like journaling will open your mind to the possibility of healing and a better future, and with that positivity comes progression. And with that progression comes change and happiness. So, whether you write novels, blogs, journals or anything else you can think of (poetry is often a favorite amongst writers too, as there's no structure and you can explore the world with your own rules) stick to it. One step at a time. One day at a time. Eventually, you'll be where you want to be.

> *"To get through the hardest journey*
> *we need take only one step at a time,*
> *but we must keep on stepping."*
> - Old Chinese Proverb.

Since the dawn of time, metaphors about taking one day at a time or one step at a time have spurred human beings on toward greatness.

causes that matter to you. All that is possible because you took the time and tools available to you to heal. The Buddha said, *"Happiness comes when your work and words are of benefit to yourself and others."* Not forgetting that whatever you do, should not be at a detriment to yourself. You are, after all, the very center of your own world, and taking care of yourself ensures that you can put lightness out into the world. We could all do with more lightness in our lives. Opening ourselves up to this, through writing, benefits not only us but the world around us.

> *"We rise by lifting others."*
> – Robert Ingersoll.

When you reach the peak of your mountain I would love for you to think of what you can do to help others and what your experience could bring to those around you. Turning the negative of wounds and scars into lightness and positivity is surely the aim of our healing. This is the final thing I wish to leave you with here. I hope you see the purpose of picking up a pen and writing, not just for yourself but for the world. We each can impact those around us in ways we never know; therefore, the journey of healing and lightness is imperative, to say the least. Being your most authentic and whole self is what the world REALY needs you to be!

The End of Our Journey

In which I hand you the pen
and send you on your way.

*"The future is completely open and we
are writing it moment to moment."*
– Pema Chödrön

Our fable ended with the words, "*I didn't have to
be afraid anymore. I was just who I am. That healing is
always available to me and that love was there for me.
I was lovable. But I needed my ladder, His special gift
of choice to me, to get to the healing. That I might use
it to go to the pit but that I didn't have to. And most
of all, it was not the ladder or the path, or the water
that was the greatest gift of all. **The greatest gift of
all was the opportunity to use them.**" And thus, this
journey, this book, ends with my passing of the ladder
(in our case a pen) to you. You have the opportunity to
use what I have shared with you; of the magical power
of writing and the healing properties it possesses. What
you choose to do with that knowledge is up to you.
Whether you go on to write the next best-selling book,
or you dive into a journal for healing, both are equally

impressive and equally valid. However you choose to use the tool of writing (your ladder to help you emerge from the hole you found yourself in) is up to you. Only you can possibly know how writing can serve you best.

Remember the quote we shared toward the beginning of the book, *"The more light you allow within you, the brighter the world you live in will be." - Shakti Gawain.* This is the mental image I would love you to take with you as you embark on your healing journey. No matter what our pasts, we should do all we can to make our inner selves light and bright. Life is too short to live in darkness and solitude. We can reside here for a short time but then we need to create a plan to carry on with our journey. Stagnation is the enemy of growth and healing. And healing comes from taking the time to enlighten ourselves about our dreams, our beliefs, and who we are. Journaling is no longer something for bored teenagers, it is a real tool for growth and change and no matter what you're writing, you will find the words you need to share. Simply by picking up the pen and putting words on the page, you'll eventually stumble upon the words you were always meant to write. The words that would lead to your healing and pursuit of the future you always dreamed of.

Happiness and healing are two things that are intrinsically individual to each and every one of us. Where I might be happy, you might not be so. Where you are happy, I might not be so. Writing provides the opportunity to look inside of yourself, without the judgment and gaze of others, and truly learn what it means for you to be happy and heal. You heal for yourself, first and foremost, and then you put out that positive healing energy into the rest of the world in whatever ways you can. To me, this is why writing is a truly mesmerizing phenomenon. Not only is writing something basic that we use to communicate with others, but it is something amazing that we can use to look inside of ourselves, heal from our pasts, and look toward our futures.

A Final Thank You from the Author

To all the readers that have taken time out of their daily lives to learn about the value of writing and the true magic it possesses, I thank you. Thank you for allowing me to share with you my knowledge as your humble guide and friend. I hope you have taken something from our fable, and something from my own personal experiences. Writing has saved my life in many ways and I would love for more people to be able to experience the sheer power of writing and journaling as I have. Whether you have past trauma, mental illness, or even great mental well-being, writing can be used as a tool both to heal and gain perspective and clarity. It is something I wish for all of you. May you go forward in your life with a renewed sense of purpose and clarity. No matter what you are going through, there is a light at the end of the tunnel. You have the tools and opportunity to make of this life what you want from it.

I wish you healing words and thoughts.